Crops

by Fred Ignacio

Illustrated with Photographs

Drawings by Katie Lee

HAMPTON-BROWN

Crops

rice

broccoli

string beans

eggplant

lettuce

carrot

chile

wheat

wheat field

banana

orange

orange grove

apple

cotton

cotton field

Crops

Six crops. Each of them is different. All are alike in some way.

Cranberries
pages 6–7

Wheat
pages 8–11

Cotton
pages 12–15

Potatoes

Oranges

Sugarcane

Cranberries

The cranberry is a little fruit
with a big taste.

The cranberry plant

Planting

The farmer plants cranberry
vines in bogs. These vines
live for many years.

Bogs are wet areas of land.

Harvesting

To harvest cranberries, farmers flood the bogs. Harvesters knock the berries off the vines. The berries float to the top of the water. Then they are gathered.

These farmers are harvesting cranberries.

Cranberry Products

Cranberries add a sharp, sweet taste to many foods.

cranberry juice

cranberry muffin

cranberry sauce

Wheat

Wheat is one of the most important crops in the world. Ten thousand years ago, people planted wheat. They used simple tools.

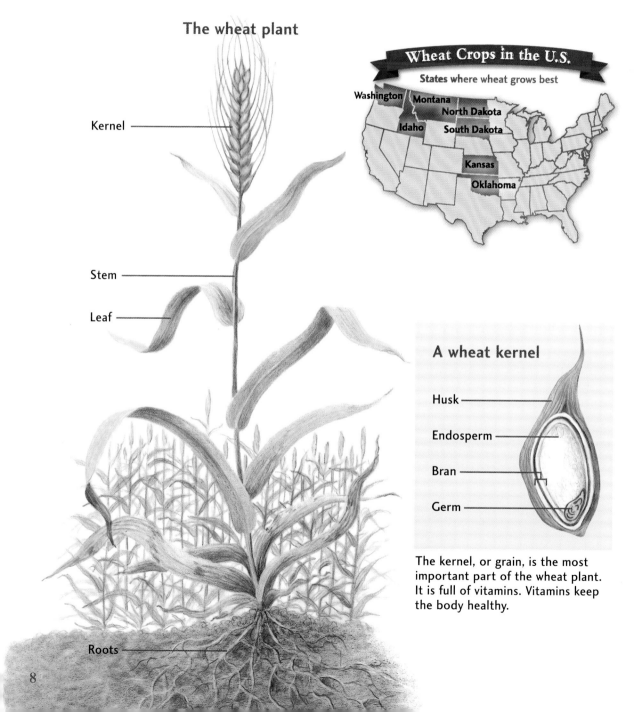

The wheat plant

Kernel

Stem

Leaf

Roots

Wheat Crops in the U.S.

States where wheat grows best

Washington
Montana
North Dakota
Idaho
South Dakota
Kansas
Oklahoma

A wheat kernel

Husk

Endosperm

Bran

Germ

The kernel, or grain, is the most important part of the wheat plant. It is full of vitamins. Vitamins keep the body healthy.

Planting

Today, wheat farmers use machines. One machine plows the fields. The plow breaks up the soil. Another machine drops seeds into the soil and covers them.

A machine called a *drill* is used to plant wheat seeds.

Protecting the Crop

Farmers need to control insects and weeds. These pests can harm crops.

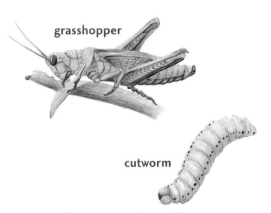

grasshopper

cutworm

thistle

wild onion

Most farmers use chemicals, or poisons, to protect their crops. These poisons kill harmful insects and weeds.

Weeds take water and food from the growing plants. Some weeds make the wheat smell bad.

9

Harvesting

Farmers use a machine to harvest the wheat. The machine cuts the stalks. Then it separates the kernels from the plant.

A machine called a *combine* is used to harvest wheat.

Farmers take the wheat to big grain elevators. The grain elevator cleans and dries the wheat. Then the wheat is sold.

The Price of Wheat

Wheat prices are always changing. Prices go up when the supply is low and the demand is high. Prices go down when the supply is high and the demand is low.

Prices Paid to Farmers for a Bushel of Wheat (60 pounds)

State	1996	1997	1998
Kansas	$4.63	$3.20	$2.55
North Dakota	$4.19	$4.00	$3.20

Wheat Products

Most people in America use wheat products every day. Everything in this photo is made from the wheat plant.

cereal

flour

boxes

straw hat

pasta

bread

colored pasta

Cotton

Cotton is cool.
Almost everyone wears it.

Cotton Crops in the U.S.
States where cotton grows best

North Carolina
California
Tennessee
Arizona
Arkansas
Texas
Georgia
Louisiana
Alabama
Mississippi

Cotton plant

The ripe cotton plant produces fibers.
Fibers are like tiny hairs. They are used
to make cloth.

A Flower Becomes a Boll

After the petals fall off the flowers, the seed pod starts to grow.

The seed pod becomes a boll. Silky fibers grow from the seeds inside the boll.

When the boll opens, the cotton is ready to harvest.

Planting

Cotton farmers plant seeds in raised beds of soil. The beds keep the seeds warm.

Sprinklers spray water over the cotton plants.

Harvesting

For many years, people picked cotton by hand.
In some countries they still do. It is hard work.
Now, most farmers in the U.S. use machines.

A cotton picker pulls cotton from the bolls.

States That Grow the Most Cotton

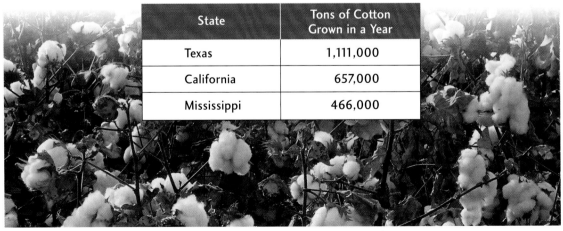

State	Tons of Cotton Grown in a Year
Texas	1,111,000
California	657,000
Mississippi	466,000

Cotton needs sunny weather. It grows best in southern regions.

Cotton Cloth

Cotton cloth is cool in the summer.
It is warm in the winter. It is soft.
It is strong. It is easy to clean.
Almost everyone wears cotton. Do you?

Weaving machine

This machine uses cotton yarn to make cloth.

Jeans are made from a cotton cloth called denim.

Other Products Made from the Cotton Plant

Every part of the cotton plant is useful.
It is used to make all these products.

swabs

yarn

cotton balls

salad dressing

cooking oil

thread

soap

Potatoes

The potato may not be pretty, but people love it. The potato is America's favorite vegetable.

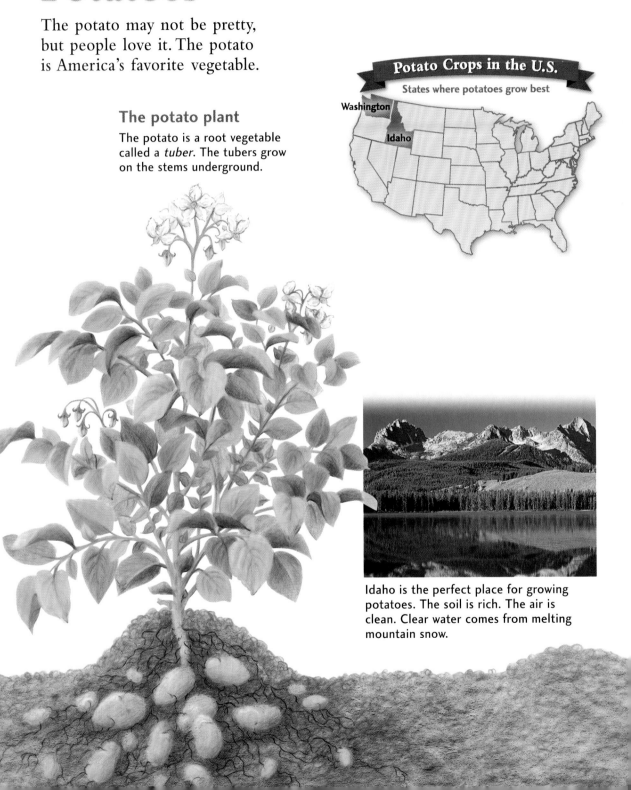

Potato Crops in the U.S.
States where potatoes grow best

Washington

Idaho

The potato plant

The potato is a root vegetable called a *tuber*. The tubers grow on the stems underground.

Idaho is the perfect place for growing potatoes. The soil is rich. The air is clean. Clear water comes from melting mountain snow.

Planting

Farmers use machines to plant seed potatoes. The machines plant up to six rows of potatoes at a time.

seed planter

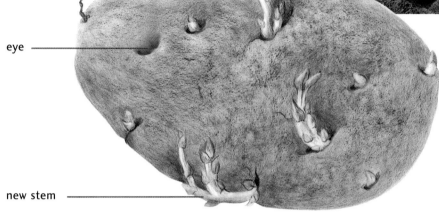

eye

new stem

Potatoes grow from small potatoes called *seed potatoes*.
Three to twenty potatoes can grow from each plant.

Cultivating

Farmers cultivate, or turn the soil, to kill weeds growing in the fields.

This tractor is pulling a machine called a *cultivator* through the potato field.

Harvesting

The farmer uses a potato combine to harvest the crop. The combine digs up the plants. It separates the potatoes and loads them into a truck.

Russet   **Yukon Gold**   **Purple**   **Red**

Potatoes come in all colors and sizes.

Fried! Baked! Boiled! Mashed! A potato tastes great no matter how you cook it.

Oranges

The orange is like a little piece of the sun. It has a sunny color and a sweet, sunny taste.

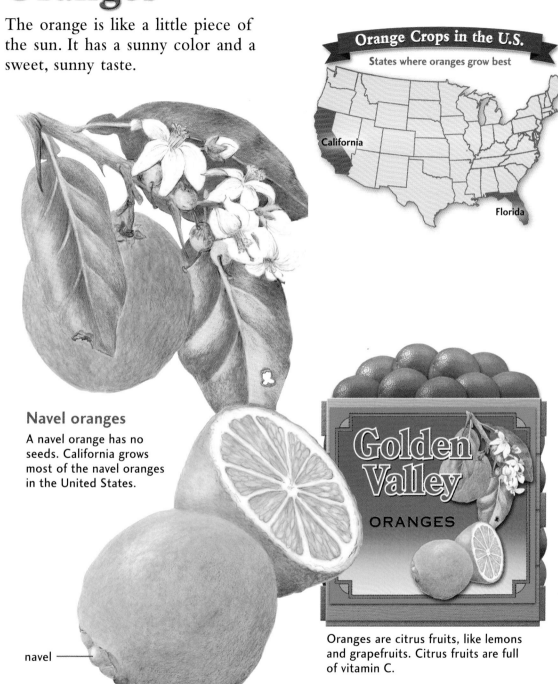

States where oranges grow best

California

Florida

Navel oranges

A navel orange has no seeds. California grows most of the navel oranges in the United States.

Golden Valley

ORANGES

navel

Oranges are citrus fruits, like lemons and grapefruits. Citrus fruits are full of vitamin C.

Planting

Orange trees are planted in groves like this.

Young trees have tubes around them. The tubes protect them from small animals.

Harvesting

Oranges are harvested by hand.

Harvesters carefully pick the oranges.

Orange Products

Oranges are mostly used to make juice. Some are sold as fresh fruit. Oils from oranges are used in foods and perfume.

perfume

marmalade

candies

orange juice

cookies

Sugarcane

All green plants produce sugar, but sugarcane produces sugar people like to eat.

Hawaii

Louisiana

Florida

The sugarcane plant

Sugarcane is a grass that grows 7 to 25 feet tall. Sweet juice is in the stalk of the sugarcane.

leaf

stalk

bud

Planting

Farmers plant sugarcane buds from the stalk. New plants grow from the buds.

Field of sugarcane in Hawaii

Harvesting

First the crop is set on fire. The fire burns off the leaves.
Then the cane is cut by hand or harvested by a machine.

The harvest fire lasts only for a few minutes. The stalks do not burn because
they have a hard shell. They also contain a lot of water.

Sugarcane Products

The biggest product from sugarcane is sugar, of course!
Now you know, farming can be sweet.

molasses

brown sugar

raw sugar

sugar cubes

granulated sugar

Six Crops

Cranberry

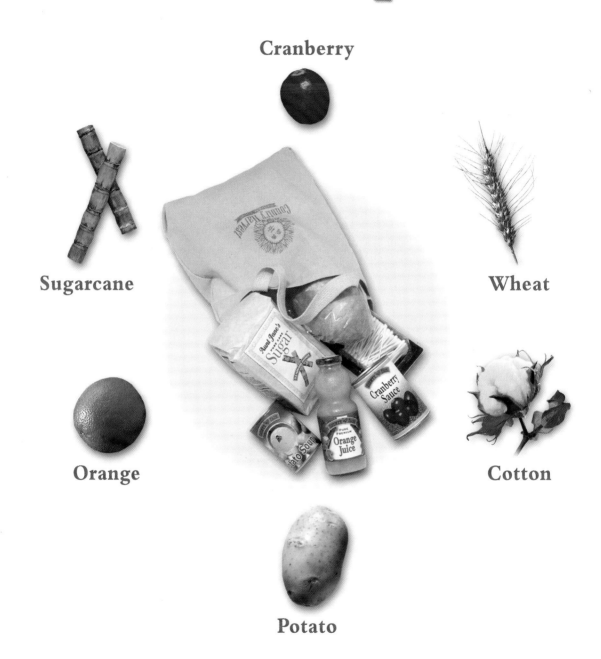

Sugarcane

Wheat

Orange

Cotton

Potato

Six crops. How is each one different? How are they all alike?